Sing to Me from the Trees, Please

Sing

Illustrations by
Rachel Heisman

to Me from the Trees, Please

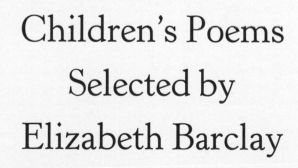

Children's Poems
Selected by
Elizabeth Barclay

The Voyager Foundation, Inc.
Washington, DC

Contents

Foreword   ROBERT LEHRMAN   7

To Our Readers, Both Acorns
  and Oaks   ELIZABETH BARCLAY   8

Poems

Up to the Treetops   ELIZABETH BARCLAY   10

Singing Time   ROSE FYLEMAN   12

Morning   BOBBI KATZ   13

Very Early   KARLA KUSKIN   14

Just Watch   MYRA COHN LIVINGSTON   16

Traffic Lights   ANONYMOUS   17

Choo-Choo   ANONYMOUS   18

The Swing   ROBERT LOUIS STEVENSON   20

Crayons: A Rainbow Poem   JANE YOLEN   22

The Tyger   WILLIAM BLAKE   24

The Frogs Wore Red Suspenders
JACK PRELUTSKY   26

Who Has Seen the Wind?   CHRISTINA
ROSSETTI   27

Every Time I Climb a Tree   DAVID MCCORD   28

Open House   AILEEN FISHER   30

Swift Things are Beautiful   ELIZABETH
COATSWORTH   31

At the Sea-Side   ROBERT LOUIS STEVENSON   32

Seal   WILLIAM JAY SMITH   33

In Just   e.e. cummings   34

Mice   ROSE FYLEMAN   36

The Purple Cow   GELETT BURGESS   37

Magic Suds   JANE MORRIS UDOVIC   38

The Question   KARLA KUSKIN   39

Trees   HARRY BEHN   40

Sometimes   JACK PRELUTSKY   42

No Worries   JANE MORRIS UDOVIC   43

Bed in Summer   ROBERT LOUIS STEVENSON   44

The Star (Twinkle, Twinkle, Little Star)
ANN AND JANE TAYLOR   45

Down from the Treetops   ELIZABETH BARCLAY   46

Good Night, Good Night   DENNIS LEE   48

Original artwork by Rachel Heisman, Annapolis, Maryland

Coordinated and edited by Terry Ann R. Neff, t.a. neff associates, inc., Tucson, Arizona
Designed and typeset by Glue + Paper Workshop, Chicago
Color separations by Embassy Graphics
Printed and bound in China through Asia Pacific Offset

NATIONAL CHILD RESEARCH CENTER

Founded in 1928, the National Child Research Center (NCRC) provides a model play-based preschool education in an inclusive environment rooted in early childhood education research. The strategic curriculum encourages and channels a child's natural inquisitiveness to foster a life-time love of learning and exploration. NCRC's teachers help develop the social-emotional tools, insight, and confidence children need to succeed in school, work, and life and to be brave and adventurous as well as kind and compassionate. NCRC is an accredited school with a diverse and inclusive, respectful community. At NCRC, there is diversity of thought, cultures, developmental needs, perspectives, and backgrounds in an atmosphere of mindfulness, kindness, character, empathy, and joy.

National Child Research Center
3209 Highland Place NW
Washington, DC 20008
202.363.8777
ncrcpreschool.org

Anonymous, "Choo-Choo"; "Traffic Lights" from *THE EVERYTHING BOOK*. © 2000 Denise Fleming. Reprinted with permission from Henry Holt and Company, LLC. All Rights Reserved.

Elizabeth Barclay, "Down from the Treetops"; "Up to the Treetops." © 2015 Elizabeth Barclay. With permission from the author.

Harry Behn, "Trees" from *THE LITTLE HILL: Poems & Pictures by Harry Behn*. © 1949 Harry Behn. © renewed 1977 by Alice L. Behn. All Rights Reserved. With permission from Marian Reiner.

Elizabeth Coatsworth, "Swift Things Are Beautiful" from *Away Goes Sally*, 1934. © 1934 The Macmillan Company. © 2003 Bethlehem Books. With permission from Bethlehem Books.

E.E. Cummings, "in just-". © 1923, 1951, 1991 the Trustees for the E.E. Cummings Trust. © 1976 George James Firmage, from *COMPLETE POEMS: 1904 – 1962 by E.E. Cummings*, ed. George J. Firmage. With permission from Liveright Publishing Corporation.

Aileen Fisher, "Open House" from *In the Wood, In the Meadow, In the Sky*, 1965. © renewed 1993 by Aileen Fisher. With permission from Marian Reiner on behalf of the Boulder Public Library Foundation, Inc.

Rose Fyleman, "Mice" © 1932 Rose Fyleman; "Singing Timez" © 1923 Rose Fyleman. With permission from The Society of Authors as the Literary Representative of the Estate of Rose Fyleman.

Bobbi Katz, "Morning" from *Upside Down and Inside Out: Poems for All Your Pockets*. © 1970 Bobbi Katz. With permission from the author who controls all rights.

Karla Kuskin, "The Question"; "Very Early" from *IN THE MIDDLE OF THE TREES*. © 1959, renewed by Karla Kuskin. With permission from Scott Treimel NY.

Dennis Lee, "Good Night, Good Night" from *Jelly Belly*. © 1983 Dennis Lee. With permission from the author.

Myra Cohn Livingston, "Just Watch" from *Whispers and Other Poems*. © 1958 Myra Cohn Livingston. © renewed 1986. With permission from Marian Reiner.

David McCord, "Every Time I Climb a Tree" from *One at a Time*, 1952. © renewed 1980 by David McCord. With permission from Little, Brown Books for Young Readers.

Jack Prelutsky, "The Frogs Wore Red Suspenders" © 1958 Jack Prelutsky; "Sometimes" © 1980 Jack Prelutsky. With permission from HarperCollins Publishers.

Public domain: William Blake, "The Tyger," 1794; Gelett Burgess, "The Purple Cow," 1895; Christina Rossetti, "Who Has Seen the Wind?," 1947; Robert Louis Stevenson, "At the Sea-Side"; "Bed in Summer"; "The Swing" from *A Child's Garden of Verses*, 1913; Ann and Jane Taylor, "The Star (Twinkle, Twinkle, Little Star)."

William Jay Smith, "Seal." Permission requested.

Jane Morris Udovic, "Magic Suds" © 2014 Jane Morris Udovic; "No Worries" © 2013 Jane Morris Udovic. With permission from the author.

Jane Yolen, "Crayons: A Rainbow Poem" from *Color Me a Rhyme*. © 2000 Jane Yolen. Published by Wordsong, an imprint of Boyds Mills Press. Reprinted by permission.

Foreword

POETRY, like nature's seasons, is both timeless and ever-changing. It is filled with different rhythms, even different colors and tones. And the children at National Child Research Center School in Washington, DC, learn about the beauty of nature and their world by exploring its many mysteries, joys, and wonders.

Liz Barclay was head of NCRC from 2008 to 2014. Each day, Liz dressed in a poetic and stylish ensemble that celebrated the spirit of the season, and she would welcome every student and parent back to school. With her radiant smile and her generous and caring ways, she brought sunshine and a warmth that reflected NCRC's goal of encouraging a lifelong love of learning.

Liz's presence is its own beautiful poetry. So, when she retired, I wanted to recognize her wonderful esprit for all the families of NCRC for generations to come. This book of poetry, selected by Liz and illustrated by her friend, Rachel Heisman, is our attempt to share Liz's love of life and poetry with the students and parents of our school—and beyond.

Liz picked these poems to encourage you to snuggle up with the children in your life and discover the magic of poetry. A good poem, like a good friend, gets better with age. With its clear images and subtle nuances, it can help us better see and appreciate the world and develop a growing love for its infinite possibilities. A poem can leave us with a feeling shared that we might never otherwise have noticed. Like the "certain slant of light" on a clear fall day, it makes the world look more beautiful. That is why we have compiled this book and that is our hope for all of our readers. Enjoy!

Robert Lehrman
NCRC Class of 1956

With lots of love to True Blue Aimee, and to JJJ and my family. May I say, in so many ways, each and every day...

You are my poetry! ~ RL

To Our Readers, Both Acorns and Oaks

SING TO ME FROM THE TREES, PLEASE is a collection of some of my favorite poems that have an appeal that reaches across all ages and times. The poems presented here are a mere sampling; a comprehensive volume of my favorites would be far too heavy to hold. These are poems both old and new; some are classics and others come from poets who are just emerging on the literary scene. Some are connected to our theme of trees; others relate to animals, playtime, or the day-to-day life of the child. Some are serious; others are sheer silliness. Each is enjoyable in its own way and was chosen with young children in mind. In addition to the words themselves, artist Rachel Heisman has responded to the selection with stunning, immersive collages that illustrate each poem, adding a deeply evocative visual dimension to enrich the experience for readers.

This book has been compiled as a gift to you so that you and the children in your life may share many happy moments enjoying poetry together. Reading aloud with children is one of the most satisfying of experiences. Snuggling with a child and a book in your lap creates a sense of warmth and security. Beyond the feeling of well-being, reading with young children promotes literacy and instills a love for sounds, images, and concepts. The words in the poems that follow dance and sing, animating and often inspiring rich ideas and emotions. The power of poetry goes well beyond the simple interpretation of a story or idea. Children learn about patterns, rhythms, and voice. They become exposed to new vocabulary and hear words used in different and uncommon ways. Because poetry strays from the concrete, it allows children to respond to the words with their own feelings and visions.

This book came about through a collaboration developed with my good friend Robert Lehrman, whom I met during my rewarding six-year headship at the National Child Research Center in Washington, DC. The children of Robert and his wife, Aimee, were students at the school. At our very first meeting, Robert and I discovered a shared love for poetry. The many discussions and communications that ensued focused on poems we both appreciated. Robert is also passionate about young children and the essential goal of a well-rounded education. When I completed my tenure, he suggested that his charitable organization, The Voyager Foundation, undertake this project. You hold the result in your hands.

It takes a village to raise a child and it takes a team to bring a project like this to fruition. First and foremost, my deepest gratitude is to Robert Lehrman himself, for his encouragement and his generosity. As mentioned above, this selection of poems would not be the same without Rachel Heisman's colorful and engaging illustrations. Elizabeth Denholm from The Voyager Foundation has done a superlative job in clearing copyright and trafficking materials; Beth Calmes helped with the logistics. Freelance consultant Terry Ann R. Neff advised on the project, edited the text, and managed all the team. Amanda Freymann and Joan Sommers of Glue + Paper Workshop took the illustrations and text and turned our good intentions into reality.

My hope is that you and the children you love will find this book to be a pleasure over and over again. Perhaps the poems will make you sing and dance! I hope you will read it together before bedtime, while traveling, on a park bench, or at the breakfast table. May your children learn from this poetry experience and remember some of these poems as their favorites, just as I do.

With fondness,
Liz Barclay

Up to the Treetops

Little seed, little sprig
Tiny tot, tender twig.

Once just a sprout
Now tall and stout.

Once just a shadow
Now like a rainbow.

Your branches so strong
Your trunk growing long.

Each season you flower
Your leaves give you power.

You grow with each day
Your heart on display.

Let's climb limb by limb
Do we dare, on a whim?

Once on top, we will stay
Read together today.

Here we are way up high,
Hugged by clouds and blue sky.

Listen well and you'll hear
Words for you, child so dear.

—ELIZABETH BARCLAY

Singing-Time

I wake in the morning early
And always, the very first thing,
I poke out my head and I sit up in bed
And I sing and I sing and I sing.

–ROSE FYLEMAN

Morning

It's Morning in the afternoon,
So eat your bacon with a spoon.
And if you have a scrambled egg,
You could feed it to your leg.

Then drink your milk up with your nose
And hop right into daddy's clothes.
Put your left shoe on your right.
It's time to start the day.
Good-night!

–BOBBI KATZ

Very Early

When I wake in the early mist
The sun has hardly shown
And everything is still asleep
And I'm awake alone.

The stars are faint and flickering.
The sun is new and shy.
And all the world sleeps quietly
Except the sun and I.

And then the noises start,
The whirrs and huffs and hums,
The birds peep out to find a worm.
The mice squeak out for crumbs,
The calf moos out to find the cow,
And taste the morning air
And everything is wide awake
And running everywhere.

The dew has dried,
The fields are warm,
The day is loud and bright,
And I'm the one who woke the sun
And kissed the stars goodnight.

–KARLA KUSKIN

Just Watch

Watch how high I'm Jumping,
Watch how far I hop,
Watch how long I'm skipping,
Watch how fast I stop!

—MYRA COHN LIVINGSTON

Traffic Lights

"Stop," says the red light,
"Go," says the green,
"Wait," says the yellow light
Blinking in between
That's what they say and
That's what they mean.
We all must obey them
Even the Queen.

–ANONYMOUS

CHOO

Now the bell is ringing,
Now the whistle blows,

What a lot of noise it makes
Everywhere it goes.

ANONYMOUS

19

The Swing

How do you like to go up in a swing,
    Up in the air so blue?
Oh, I do think it the pleasantest thing
    Ever a child can do!

Up in the air and over the wall,
    Till I can see so wide,
Rivers and trees and cattle and all
    Over the countryside—

Till I look down on the garden green,
    Down on the roof so brown—
Up in the air I go flying again,
    Up in the air and down!

–ROBERT LOUIS STEVENSON

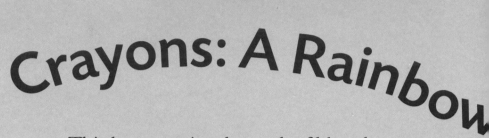

Crayons: A Rainbow

This box contains the wash of blue sky,
spikes of green spring,
a circle of yellow sun,
triangle flames of orange and red.

It has the lime caterpillar
inching on a brown branch,
the shadow black in the center
of a grove of trees.

It holds my pink
and your chocolate
and her burnt sienna
and his ivory skin.
In it are all the colors of the world.
All the colors of the world.

—JANE YOLEN

Poem

The Tyger

Tyger Tyger, burning bright,
In the forests of the night;
What immortal hand or eye,
Could frame thy fearful symmetry?

In what distant deeps or skies.
Burnt the fire of thine eyes?
On what wings dare he aspire?
What the hand, dare seize the fire?

And what shoulder, & what art,
Could twist the sinews of thy heart?
And when thy heart began to beat,
What dread hand? & what dread feet?

What the hammer? what the chain,
In what furnace was thy brain?
What the anvil? what dread grasp,
Dare its deadly terrors clasp!

When the stars threw down their spears
And water'd heaven with their tears:
Did he smile his work to see?
Did he who made the Lamb make thee?

Tyger Tyger burning bright,
In the forests of the night:
What immortal hand or eye,
Dare frame thy fearful symmetry?

–WILLIAM BLAKE

The Frogs Wore Red Suspenders

The frogs wore red suspenders
And the pigs wore purple vests,
As they sang to all the chickens
And ducks upon their nests.

They croaked and oinked a serenade,
The ducks and chickens sighed,
Then laid enormous spangled eggs,
And quacked and clucked with pride.

—JACK PRELUTSKY

Who Has Seen the Wind?

Who has seen the wind?
Neither I nor you:
But when the leaves hang trembling,
The wind is passing through.

Who has seen the wind?
Neither you nor I:
But when the trees bow down their heads,
The wind is passing by.

—CHRISTINA ROSSETTI

27

Every Time I Climb a Tree

Every time I climb a tree
Every time I climb a tree
Every time I climb a tree
I scrape a leg
Or skin a knee
And every time I climb a tree
I find some ants
Or dodge a bee
And get the ants
All over me.

And every time I climb a tree
Where have you been?
They say to me
But don't they know that I am free
Every time I climb a tree?

I like it best
To spot a nest
That has an egg
Or maybe three.

And then I skin
The other leg
But every time I climb a tree
I see a lot of things to see
Swallows rooftops and TV
And all the fields and farms there be
Every time I climb a tree
Though climbing may be good for ants
It isn't awfully good for pants
But still it's pretty good for me
Every time I climb a tree

—DAVID MCCORD

29

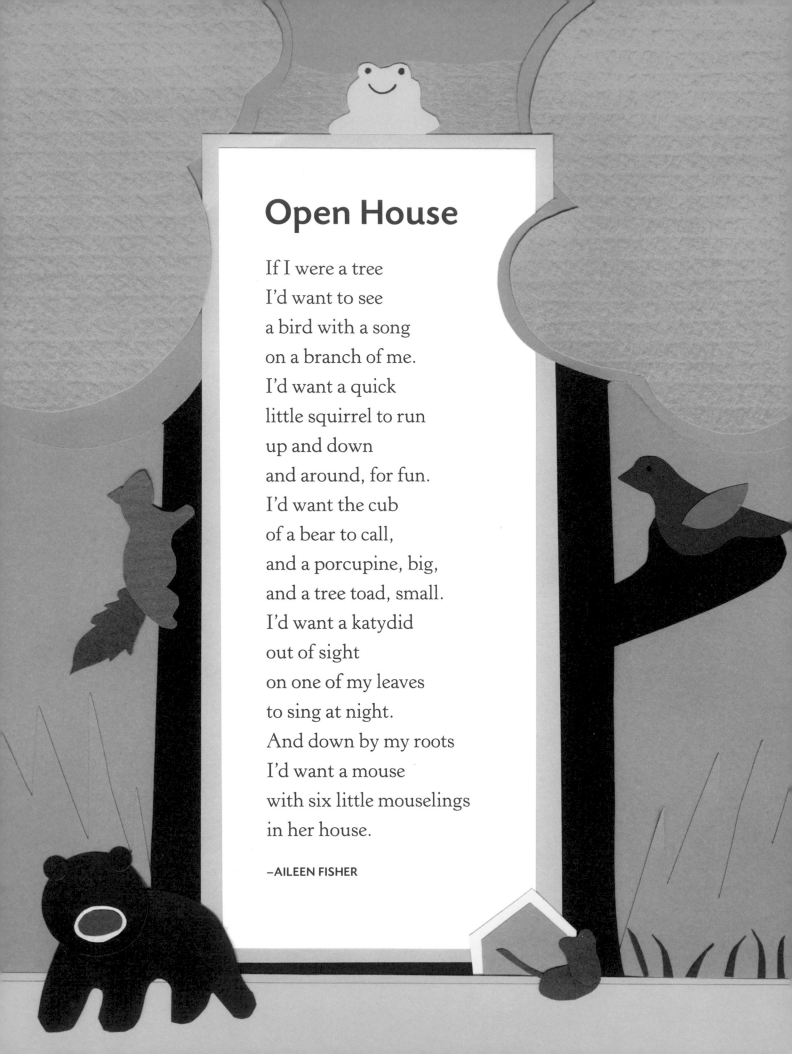

Open House

If I were a tree
I'd want to see
a bird with a song
on a branch of me.
I'd want a quick
little squirrel to run
up and down
and around, for fun.
I'd want the cub
of a bear to call,
and a porcupine, big,
and a tree toad, small.
I'd want a katydid
out of sight
on one of my leaves
to sing at night.
And down by my roots
I'd want a mouse
with six little mouselings
in her house.

–AILEEN FISHER

Swift Things
Are Beautiful

Swift things are beautiful:
Swallows and deer,
And lightening that falls
Bright-veined and clear,
Rivers and meteors,
Wind in the wheat,
The strong-withered horse,
The runner's sure feet.

And slow things are beautiful:
The closing of day,
The pause of the wave
That curves downward to spray,
The ember that crumbles,
The opening flower,
And the ox that moves on
In the quiet of power.

—ELIZABETH COATSWORTH

At the Sea-Side

When I was down beside the sea
A wooden spade they gave to me
   To dig the sandy shore.
My holes were empty like a cup.
In every hole the sea came up
   Till it could come no more.

–ROBERT LOUIS STEVENSON

Seal

See how he dives
 From the rocks with a zoom!
  See how he darts
   Through his watery room
   Past crabs and eels
  And green seaweed,
 Past fluffs of sandy
Minnow feed!
See how he swims
 With a swerve and a twist,
  A flip of the flipper,
   A flick of the wrist!
   Quicksilver-quick,
  Softer than spray,
 Down he plunges
And sweeps away;
Before you can think,
 Before you can utter
  Words like "Dill pickle"
   Or "Apple butter,"
   Back up he swims
  Past Sting Ray and Shark,
 Out with a zoom,
A whoop, a bark;
Before you can say
 Whatever you wish,
  He plops at your side
   With a mouthful of fish!

—WILLIAM JAY SMITH

in just–

in Just–
spring   when the world is mud–
luscious the little
lame balloonman

whistles   far   and wee

and eddieandbill come
     running from marbles and
          piracies and it's
               spring

when the world is puddle-wonderful

     the queer
          old balloonman whistles
               far   and   wee
          and bettyandisbel come dancing

     from hop-scotch and jump-rope and

it's
spring
and

the

goat-footed

balloonMan   whistles
far

and

wee

–E.E. CUMMINGS

Mice

I think mice
are nice.

Their tails are long
Their faces small,
They haven't any
Chins at all.

Their ears are pink,
Their teeth are white,
They run about
The house at night.

They nibble things
They shouldn't touch
And no one seems
To like them much.

But *I* think mice
Are nice

–ROSE FYLEMAN

36

The Purple Cow

I never saw a Purple Cow,
I never hope to see one;
But I can tell you, anyhow,
I'd rather see than be one.

—GELETT BURGESS

Magic Suds

The shower sprinkles sparkling rain
Upon my shampooed head.
And, as it washes off the suds,
It changes some instead
Into a frothy potion that
Invigorates my brain,
While all the other soapy suds
Go trickling down the drain.
The magic suds massage my brain
And tickle every part.
I think that is the reason why
I am so very smart!

–JANE MORRIS UDOVIC

The Question

People always say to me
"What do you think you'd like to be
When you grow up?"
And I say, "Why,
I think I'd like to be the sky
Or be a plane or train or mouse
Or maybe a haunted house
Or something furry, rough and wild . . .
Or maybe I will stay a child."

–KARLA KUSKIN

Trees

Trees are the kindest things I know,
They do no harm, they simply grow
And spread a shade for sleepy cows,
And gather birds among their bows.

They give us fruit in leaves above,
And wood to make our houses of,
And leaves to burn on Halloween
And in the Spring new buds of green.

They are first when day's begun
To tough the beams of morning sun,
They are the last to hold the light
When evening changes into night.

And when a moon floats on the sky
They hum a drowsy lullaby
Of sleepy children long ago . . .
Trees are the kindest things I know.

—HARRY BEHN

Sometimes

Sometimes I simply have to cry,
I don't know why,
I don't know why.
There's really nothing very wrong.
I probably should sing a song
or run around and make some noise
or sit and tinker with my toys
or pop a couple of balloons
or play a game or watch cartoons,
but I'm feeling sad,
though I don't know why,
and all I want to do is cry.

–JACK PRELUTSKY

No Worries!

What if I start on the wrong foot? *I'll throw in a hop as I skip*

What if I pedal in circles? *I might have an interesting trip!*

What if I can't hit the high notes? *I'll make up a song on my own.*

What if I trip on my big feet? *At least I can see that I've grown.*

What if I lose things I've hidden? *A treasure hunt works like a charm.*

What if I step in a puddle? *I'm barefoot—no need for alarm.*

Clearly, I'll never be perfect

Since perfect is too hard to be.

That's why I'm happy-go-lucky

And why I'm the happiest me.

–JANE MORRIS UDOVIC

Bed in Summer

In winter I get up at night
And dress by yellow candle-light.
In summer, quite the other way,
I have to go to bed by day.

I have to go to bed and see
The birds still hopping on the tree,
Or hear the grown-up people's feet
Still going past me in the street.

And does it not seem hard to you,
When all the sky is clear and blue,
And I should like so much to play,
To have to go to bed by day?

–ROBERT LOUIS STEVENSON

The Star

Twinkle, twinkle, little star,
How I wonder what you are!
Up above the world so high,
Like a diamond in the sky.

When the blazing sun is gone,
When he nothing shines upon,
Then you show your little light,
Twinkle, twinkle, all the night.

Then the trav'ller in the dark,
Thanks you for your tiny spark,
He could not see which way to go,
If you did not twinkle so.

In the dark blue sky you keep,
And often thro' my curtains peep,
For you never shut your eye,
Till the sun is in the sky.

'Tis your bright and tiny spark,
Lights the trav'ller in the dark :
Tho' I know not what you are,
Twinkle, twinkle, little star.

–ANN AND JANE TAYLOR

Down from the Treetops

Can you peek through the trees?
See the sun on its knees?

Smell the night closing in?
Feel the chill on your chin?

Let your eyes lose the light,
You can see it is night.

The bees and the ants,
The weeds we don't plant.

The owls in the trees,
And a soft, silent breeze.

They all say it's time,
For us to un-climb.

Down to the ground,
Where we land, not a sound.

So we tip-toe to bed,
Where we lay fast our head.

And we hear just a hush,
Our day now at dusk.
Nighty night, time for still
Time to grow and you will.

–ELIZABETH BARCLAY

Good Night, Good Night

The dark is dreaming.
Day is done.
Good night, good night
To everyone.
Good night to the birds,
And the fish in the sea
Good night to the bears
And good night to me.

–DENNIS LEE